DIVIDE AND CONQUER:
Responsible Security
for America's Poor

DIVIDE AND CONQUER: Responsible Security for America's Poor

by David T. Ellwood*

SCHOOL OF
CALIFORNIA
PROFESSIONAL
PSYCHOLOGY
LOS ANGELES

Occasional Paper Number One
Ford Foundation Project on
Social Welfare and the American Future

* David T. Ellwood is an associate professor of public
policy at the John F. Kennedy School of Government,
Harvard University.

One of a series of reports on activities supported by the Ford Foundation. A complete list of publications may be obtained from the Ford Foundation, Office of Reports, 320 East 43 Street, New York, New York 10017.

Library of Congress Cataloging-in-Publication Data

Ellwood, David T., 1987
  Divide and conquer

  (Occasional paper / Ford Foundation Project on Social Welfare and the American Future; no. 1)
  Includes bibliographical references.
  1. Poor—United States. 2. Child welfare—United States. 3. Family policy—United States. 4. Income maintenance programs—United States. I. Title. II. Series: Occasional paper (Ford Foundation. Project on Social Welfare and the American Future; no. 1)
HV91.E45 1987   362.5'8'0973   87-23621
ISBN:0-916584-31-3

EXECUTIVE PANEL
Ford Foundation Project on Social
Welfare and the American Future

Contents

Foreword

The United States has a two-pronged system of social welfare—one that is designed for labor-force participants and the other for those who do not work. For workers, a combination of employee benefit and government social insurance programs provides protection against the risks of illness, disability, and unemployment and also sets aside funds for income maintenance and health coverage during the retirement years. Nonworkers, mainly children, the disabled, and the elderly, are sustained by a governmental safety net program. Except for low-income single parents with young children, able-bodied, working-age adults are expected to work and thereby provide for their needs.

Does this social welfare system, designed in large part in the 1930s, provide sufficient protection for Americans as they are about to enter the 21st century? Have significant holes developed in the fabric of social protection, and, if so, is society willing to pay for mending them? Has the changing composition of the U.S. population, specifically the increase in the elderly and single-parent families, altered the premises on which the system was built? Why is there such a persistently high level of poverty, in good times and bad, and can anything be done to correct it? Can more be done to help the troubling number of American children who experience at least some poverty in their growing-up years?

These are some of the questions that the Ford Foundation set out to answer when in 1985 it launched a wide-ranging inquiry into alternative approaches to providing social insurance and welfare services, taking into account changes in the economy, in the family and work, and in the nation's age profile. Called the Project on Social Welfare and the American Future, the inquiry is led by a twelve-member executive panel of citizens representing the business, academic, civil rights, and labor communities.* Chairman of the panel is Irving S. Shapiro, until recently a member of the Foundation's Board of Trustees and a former chief executive officer of the du Pont Company.

In the course of its inquiry, the panel has commissioned a number of research reports and convened sessions of social policy experts to discuss approaches to such interrelated topics as health care, retirement and pension policy, poverty and welfare policy, and public and private social welfare programs. For one of the sessions, in November 1986, the panel invited leading scholars and practitioners in the field of poverty and welfare to discuss the policy implications of their work. They were asked to address three topics: the diverse and interrelated causes of poverty, the consequences of poverty for individuals and society as a whole, and whether the safety net and training programs developed since the 1930s are appropriate for fighting poverty in the 1980s and beyond.

Together with several specially commissioned research reports, the papers offer an unusually comprehensive picture of why people are poor and what has been and might be done about it. For this reason, the Foundation has decided to publish them, beginning with David Ellwood's review of our various income-maintenance programs and Judith Gueron's paper on how the welfare system might be reformed. Other papers will follow. They include discussions of the current social protection system and its shortcomings; of the macroeconomic, behavioral, and human capital explanations

---

* Members of the panel are listed on page *v.*

for poverty; of the potential of new management approaches to improve the efficiency of government social programs; and the role of health care, child support, education, training, and tax incentives in reducing different kinds of poverty. The views expressed in the papers are the authors' own and do not necessarily reflect those of members of the executive panel or of the staff and board of the Ford Foundation.

We are grateful to the authors for taking time out from their busy schedules to set down their thoughts on a complex range of issues. Together they have made a useful contribution to the current debate over social welfare policy.

Franklin A. Thomas
President
Ford Foundation

Introduction

Charles Murray has created quite a stir. He has written a powerful indictment of the whole social welfare system.* According to Murray, the very system designed to help the poor has instead created dependent wards by penalizing the virtuous and rewarding the dysfunctional. Much of Murray's book is a graphical and statistical analysis of what has happened to the poor in general and to the black poor in particular. Much of the power of his case comes from the fact that he looks at two very fundamental questions: Why are people poor? Does our social welfare system reflect and reinforce our basic values?

The intellectual establishment, particularly the liberal intellectual establishment, has been quick to attack Murray's statistical work. These attacks cast considerable doubt on the credibility of Murray's conclusions. But what is often missed in this frenzy is that although Murray may have gotten the answers wrong, he probably got the questions right.

Unfortunately, Murray fell into much the same trap that social reformers have slipped into for centuries. Though he paid lip service to the diversity of the poor, he ultimately ignored the extremely heterogeneous nature of this group and of the causes of poverty. In reading his book, one is left thinking only of a black underclass trapped by its own counter-culture, which is nourished by social policies that avoid "blaming the victim."

---

* Murray, Charles A., *Losing Ground: American Social Policy* (New York: Basic Books, 1984).

1

Yet *less than 10 percent of America's poor are minorities living in severe poverty areas in our major cities.* Murray's reader misses entirely the poverty of West Virginia, where unemployment rates often exceed 18 percent and families express great satisfaction with workfare programs. One easily forgets the recently divorced women who use welfare as transitional assistance until they can support themselves. Also absent is any discussion of the working poor, particularly those persons who are working full time but are still poor. And Murray's readers may fail to notice that the bulk of our resources are devoted to aiding the elderly and disabled, not the healthy laggard.

The poor have always been viewed in stereotypical terms; it seems that such stereotypes are inevitable in political discussions. They are certainly critical for those who attempt to "solve the poverty problem" with simple, all-encompassing solutions. Just as Murray pointed to the "underclass" as a justification for eliminating most of our social welfare system, the advocates of the negative income tax focused on the working poor to justify a program that provided support to the entire poor population.

The country has been ill-served by such simplifications. By lumping together all the poor into one or another category, one is faced with programmatic compromises and philosophical conundrums. How can we be generous to those who cannot work yet still reward and encourage those who can and do work? A program that treats unemployed teenagers in the same way as disabled, middle-aged adults if their incomes match will likely serve both groups poorly. When "the poor" are a single class, the oldest questions of inherent human nature surface. Is poverty voluntary? Are the poor taking sufficient responsibility for themselves? Does welfare corrupt?

There are many situations in which these questions need not arise. Disability certified by a doctor is unlikely to be voluntary. Someone working full time can hardly be expected to do more. A family that uses welfare for temporary assistance probably has not been corrupted. There are cases in which these difficult questions must be faced, but even then the issues look very different in specific situations than they do in the abstract.

In this paper, which is drawn largely from a forthcoming book to be published by Basic Books, I will consider both the reasons for poverty and the value questions these reasons pose.[1] The paper addresses only the poverty of families with children, for it is these families that inspire the greatest empathy and concern. It is my conclusion that by dividing the poor into a few groups and by recognizing the several reasons why people are poor, one can piece together a system of income support that is both more effective in reducing poverty and more compatible with the basic values that now occupy so much political discussion. What my colleague Mary Jo Bane has called the "divide and conquer" strategy offers far more room for common ground than any of the superficially appealing "ultimate solutions."

I offer the outlines of a "responsible security" plan for families that is derived from explicit consideration of responsibility and work. It is also designed to enhance the economic security and independence of the poor by putting them in a position in which they can be essentially self-supporting without relying on welfare-like assistance. The goal is to create a system that gives both to the poor and to poverty policies the respect that comes from being in the mainstream. Indeed, RESPECT (RESPonsible sECuriTy) might be an appropriate acronym for the plan.

I argue that when one looks at the causes of poverty and seeks policies that are more in line with our values, there are strong arguments for moving toward a system that can be summarized in the following four prescriptive propositions:

• People who are already doing as much work as society deems acceptable ought to be able to support their families at or above the poverty level without relying on welfare or welfare-like supports.
• People who are poor and are not working as much as society would hope ought to be offered short-term transitional

assistance. This would include short-term cash income
coupled with training and with services designed to help them
become self-supporting.
• Long-term income maintenance for people not working as
much as society would hope ought to be provided in the form
of jobs and work, not in the form of cash welfare of indefinite
duration.
• Absent parents ought to be required to share any income
that they have with their children.

Though any talk of values often carries the taint of judg-
ment and arrogance, one cannot discuss poverty without con-
sidering responsibility and expectations. It is appropriate to
ask about the responsibilities of citizens for themselves, and
the responsibility of government to the citizens. These are
not always easy questions, but they inevitably underlie policy
debates. Only those who contend that society can expect
nothing from the poor or those who believe the poor are whol-
ly responsible for their condition can skirt these difficult
questions.

Much of this paper will be an examination of who is poor,
how long people are poor, why they are poor, and what we
now do to help deal with their poverty. I begin by looking
at the poverty of children, exploring its frequency and duration. That examination shows that the poverty experienced
by children living with two parents is dramatically different
from that of children living only with their mother. The remainder of the paper examines the problems of these two
groups separately. For each one, the nature and causes of
poverty, society's notion of responsibility, and the appropriate
policies differ significantly.

Growing Up Poor
in America

The federal government reports that in 1984 just over 20 percent of all children lived in a family that had cash income, including government cash transfers (hereafter called "transfers"), that fell below the poverty line for a family of that size. (The poverty line for the increasingly mythical family of four was $10,609.) These children were almost equally divided between homes headed by women and those headed by men. And 45 percent of the children were black, Hispanic, or members of some other minority group.

These sterile statistics fail to tell very much about the lives of these children. They miss entirely whether this poverty is temporary or permanent. They give no hint about what these children's past has been like or what can be expected in the future. Of course, it is impossible to know for sure what will happen to today's poor children. But it is possible to look at children who were born far enough in the past to determine how many and which ones actually grew up poor, and how many simply touched poverty for a short time.

Using longitudinal data from the Panel Study of Income Dynamics,[2] we can look at a single cohort of children born around 1970[3] and ask how many of them actually grew up impoverished. Table 1 provides such information. In generating this table, I excluded all government transfer income (including welfare, Social Security), so that it shows how many children were in homes where the private sources of income were insufficient to provide support above the poverty line.

Table 1

The Poverty Experiences of Children Born in
a Typical Year Around 1970*

Never Poor	Tempor- arily Poor (1-3 Yrs)	Half-Time Poor (4-6 Yrs)	Long-Term Poor (7-10 Yrs)	TOTAL
2,278	686	269	267	3,500
65.1%	19.6%	7.7%	7.6%	100.0%

* Number of children (in thousands) and percent distribution by number
of years poor in the first ten years of life.

The table shows, for example, that of the 3,500,000 children
born in an average year around 1970, 2,278,000 or 65.1 percent avoided poverty altogether in their first ten years of life.
And of those who experienced some poverty, the majority
were touched by it only briefly. One child in six was poor
for at least half of his or her early childhood; one in thirteen
literally grew up poor.

The "small" group that is hit hardest looms much larger
when we realize that the 7.6 percent of children who grew
up poor actually endured 50 percent of the poverty years experienced by children. The reason is simple enough. One child
poor for ten years experiences as much poverty as ten children
who are poor for one year. This is not statistical mumbo jum-
bo. In a very real sense the long-term poor represent half
of the poverty problem.

The notion that 7.6 percent of all children could account
for half of all the poverty—even though they are only a small
portion of all the children who ever became poor at some
point in their lives—may seem confusing. But it should not
be. Poverty is no different from all sorts of activities. Most
adults have tried cigarettes at some time in their lives, but

the bulk of the smoking is done by (and most of the cigarettes are sold to) a much smaller number who smoke a pack or two per day. Many people have been to church, but it is a tinier group of regular members who fill the pews on most days. So it is with the poverty of our children. Many have been exposed to it, but a few account for the bulk of the problem.

Policy must thus wrestle with the fact that many families suffer short-term poverty and could be helped by short-term assistance, while a few suffer longer-term problems and need help with long-term income maintenance. It may make sense to separate short-term, transitional assistance for the many from the longer-term maintenance for the few who account for so much poverty.

Who are these poor children, and what is the story of their families? We can only guess at the details when we use such abstract data. What we can do, though, is look to see if there are common features of their lives that might explain their problems. When we look for these characteristics, several stand out. Education has some relevance, though less than many would suppose. Region provides some information. Race is a powerful factor. But one characteristic dwarfs all the others in predicting poverty experiences: family structure.

Poverty and Family

Let us perform a simple thought experiment. We wish to consider the situation faced by three different children. All we know is that the first one spent his entire first ten years in a two-parent household, the second spent some part of those years in a single-parent home and the remainder in a two-parent home, and the third was born into and remained in a single-parent household. Knowing only these facts, what can we say about the likely poverty experiences of these children?

A great deal. Some 80 percent of the children in stable two-parent homes would escape poverty altogether. And only 2 percent would be long-term poor. For children in this group, poverty is uncommon, and when it occurs, it tends to be short-lived. By contrast, only 7 percent of the children who grew up entirely in single-parent homes would escape poverty, and an astonishing 62 percent would be poor during their entire first ten years of life! Here poverty is virtually guaranteed, and it is likely to last throughout childhood. For those who spend part of their childhood in homes headed by women, the results are mixed. Two-thirds will experience some poverty, but "only" 12 percent will "grow up poor."

The role of family is featured in Table 2, which shows that some 2.0 million of the 3.5 million children born in a typical year around 1970 spent their entire first ten years in two-parent[4] homes and experienced no poverty. Another 340,000 were in two-parent homes but experienced temporary poverty, and so forth.

9

Table 2

Extent of Poverty and Type of Living Situation During the First Ten Years of Childhood*

	Never Poor	Temporarily Poor (1-3 Yrs)	Half-Time Poor (4-6 Yrs)	Long-Term Poor (7-10 Yrs)	TOTAL
Always in a Two-Parent Family**	2,005	340	110	50	2,505
Some Years in a Female-Headed Family	259	321	116	92	788
Always in a Female-Headed Family	14	25	43	125	207
TOTAL	2,278	686	269	267	3,500

* For children born in a typical year in the late 1960s or early 1970s (numbers in thousands).
** The small number of single-parent male-headed families are included in this category.
Source: Special Tabulations of the Panel Study of Income Dynamics (PSID).

Several features of this table deserve special emphasis. It is unusual for children to be raised entirely in a female-headed home (only 200,000 children or 6 percent of this cohort was), yet that group accounts for almost half of all the children who are long-term poor. And most of the other long-term poor children spent part of their lives in single-parent homes. The children who literally grow up poor in America almost always spend at least part of their childhood in a female-headed home. Long-term poverty is intimately related to family structure. Even among the short-term poor, more than half spend some part of their childhood in a single-parent home.

Still, one should not come away from these figures with the impression that poverty is only a matter of family structure. On the contrary, returning to Table 2, one can calculate that 44 percent of all the children who were ever poor in their first ten years of life were always in two-parent households. And many of the children who spent only part of their lives in two-parent homes and who knew some poverty experienced some of their poverty years during the period when they lived with two parents. Indeed, financial problems such as unemployment of the husband or wife might lead the family to be poor and might contribute to the breakup of two-parent homes. In such cases, a child may spend part of his or her childhood in a single-parent home because the two-parent family was poor.

Perhaps the most striking feature of all in this table is the large proportion of our children who do not fit the image of a typical American child: one raised in a stable and prosperous (never poor) two-parent home. Only 57 percent (2,005 out of 3,500) of the children born around 1970 were never poor and never in a single-parent family.[5] And that trend is escalating for children born today. The divorce rate and the fraction of all children born to unmarried women are both much higher than they were in 1970. Most estimates now suggest that more than half of the children born today will spend some part of their lives in single-parent homes. Many others will experience poverty while in two-parent homes.

Children born today face a double threat. They face the possibility that their families will be poor at least for some period even if they remain intact. And they face the possibility that they will spend part or all of their childhood in single-parent families, in which case they will very likely experience poverty along with whatever other hardships the situation implies. A declining minority will live their lives entirely in non-poor two-parent homes. The question yet to be addressed is whether our society and its social policy institutions recognize this fact.

The Poverty of
Two-Parent Families

Roughly 9 percent of two-parent families with children are poor in any one year. If the family remains intact, we have seen that the poverty will typically be short-lived. Only one child in 50 raised in a stable two-parent home will be long-term poor, before government transfers. The causes of two-parent poverty are surprisingly easy to identify. Low pay, lack of jobs, and disability are the overwhelming problems. This claim may sound like liberal soft-headedness, but the evidence in favor of this proposition is overwhelming. Consider first what the poor themselves say when asked why they do not work more (see Table 3).

Some 28 percent of all poor husbands and 8 percent of poor wives already work more than full time throughout the year. Thus at least one adult is already working fully in one-third of poor two-parent families with children. For them the problem is simple: low wages. In spite of working all the time, they do not bring in enough money to keep the family above the poverty line. Some of these families live in rural areas; others have many children. But the fact is that if a worker works full time all year at the minimum wage, he or she will not earn enough to keep even a two-person family above the poverty line. To support a family of four, one must earn 60 percent above the minimum wage.

The table shows that unemployment is roughly of equal significance. Some 35 percent of husbands and 10 percent of wives report that they were unable to find work. Should

Table 3

Main Reasons Husbands and Wives in
Pre-Transfer Poor* Families with Children
Did Not Work More Weeks During 1984

	*Husbands** in Poor Families*	*Wives in Poor Families*
Already Working Full Year		
Full Time	28%	8%
Part Time	4%	6%
Unable to Find Work		
Worked Part Year	27%	6%
Did Not Work At All	8%	4%
Ill or Disabled	17%	5%
Retired	7%	1%
In School	3%	2%
Taking Care of Home or Family	1%	65%
Other	6%	3%
TOTAL	100%	100%

* Family income not counting government transfers is below the poverty
line.
** Includes the small number of male family heads where no wife is
present.
Source: Special Tabulations of the Current Population Survey 1984.

these claims be believed? There is much evidence to support
them. The overwhelming majority of these people worked
part of the year, which suggests that they were willing to work.
More convincingly, the number of people claiming unemployment as the cause of their poverty drops precipitously when
the overall state of the economy improves. In 1983, when the
overall unemployment rate was nearly 10 percent, 934,000
poor male heads of families reported unemployment as the
chief reason they had low earnings. In 1978, when the
unemployment rate was 6 percent (still high by historical stan-
dards), just 341,000 reported unemployment as the cause.[6]

The third reason for not working more is illness or
disability—and was reported by 17 percent of husbands and

5 percent of wives. There is other evidence to support many of their claims. The majority of those reporting illness or disability report receiving Social Security or Supplemental Security benefits, which are available only to those whom a government-approved doctor has certified as "permanently and totally disabled."[7] And the number of families reporting illness and disability does *not* vary much with overall economic conditions, suggesting that people are not using illness as an excuse for their inability to find work.

If low pay and unemployment really are the primary causes of poverty among male-headed families and if illness rates remain roughly constant over time, then one would expect that the poverty rate for children in two-parent families could be predicted in any year on the basis of overall average wages in the economy and the unemployment rate for that year. Figure 1 shows the results of such a prediction.[8] The poverty rate is forecast using only the median income of full-year, full-time male workers and the overall unemployment rate. The figure shows a perfect match. In the 1960s when real wages were rising fast and unemployment fell, poverty decreased sharply. In the 1970s when earnings were largely unchanged (after adjusting for inflation), poverty changed little. And in the 1980s when the economy turned sour, the poverty rate rose.

Contrary to the claims of Charles Murray and others, there is nothing mysterious or suggestive about the lack of progress on poverty among two-parent families in the 1970s and 1980s. This is the group for whom "trickle down" really does work. When the economy booms and wages grow while unemployment falls, this group is carried with the tide. During the 1960s wages grew and unemployment fell, and poverty dropped sharply. But starting in the early 1970s the economy was essentially stagnant, so there was nothing to trickle down. In the 1980s the economy turned quite bad, and quite predictably poverty grew rapidly. One need not look to complex explanations about the decline in manufacturing or the changing structure of the economy to explain the poverty of the 1970s and 1980s. One need only look at the whole economic picture.

Figure 1

Actual and Expected Poverty Rates for Children in Male-Headed Families

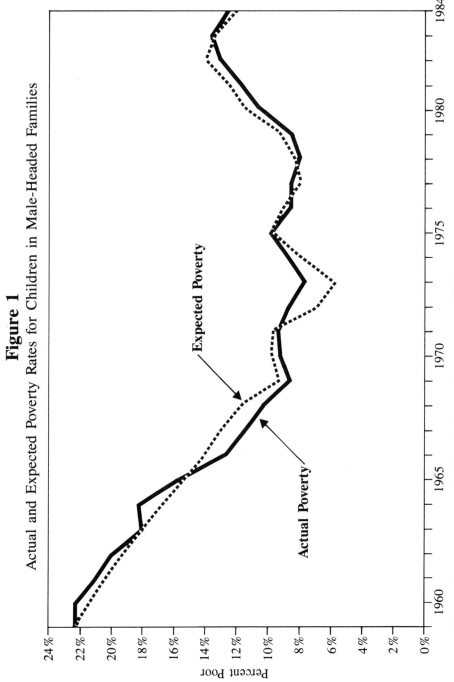

Expected poverty is based solely on the median earnings of full-year,
full-time male workers and the unemployment rate.

If the growth of the 1960s had persisted into the 1970s, the poverty rate for children in male-headed homes could easily be below 4 percent (leaving poor only those in households with adults who are disabled or unemployed). Even today in Massachusetts where the economy is booming and the unemployment rate is 3.6 percent, the pre-transfer poverty rate among two-parent families is under 5.9 percent as opposed to 11.8 percent nationally. After counting government transfers, the Massachusetts poverty rate is just 3.7 percent compared to the national average of 9.1 percent.

Should We Expect More from the Poor?

To answer such a question, one must decide what it is reasonable to expect. The question of responsibility is this: What level of work should be necessary for two-parent families to reach the society's minimal standard of living without having to rely on welfare-like support? Or more simply, what level of work should it take for a family to be minimally self-supporting?

One possible answer would be that one parent ought to work fully and a second should work partially. That is the situation in the "typical" two-parent American family now. Yet is this an appropriate standard for all families attempting to reach the poverty line? There remains considerable debate among both parents and child development specialists about the importance of having a young child cared for by a parent at home. Moreover, day care can be quite costly and difficult to obtain. And opportunities for many women remain very limited. Given the difficult position that women and families are in, particularly poor families, I believe that full-year, full-time work by one family member ought to be sufficient to reach minimal income levels in our society.

There is no question that these families share mainstream American values. They work long and hard at jobs that pay so poorly that they cannot even keep the family above the poverty line. Saying that one-worker families ought to be able to achieve the poverty level ought not to be taken as a signal that society should not pursue day care or increased oppor-

19

tunities for women. It is merely a statement about our society's minimum expectations for families, given the current set of opportunities and options. And if two-parent families wanted to improve their economic position beyond the poverty level, then they could do what many middle-class families do: send two people into the labor force.

In one-third of all poor (pre-transfer) two-parent households either the husband or wife (the husband in most cases) works full year full time. In another 10 percent of these homes, the combined work of the husband and wife exceeds the equivalent of one full-year full-time worker. Thus roughly 40 percent of our poor two-parent families cannot possibly be judged "irresponsible" or outside the mainstream.

Another group for which there is little doubt about responsibility is the disabled. If someone is unable to work because of illness or disability, he or she cannot, by definition, be expected to work. In perhaps 20 percent of poor two-parent homes, either the husband or wife reports that illness or disability prevents him or her from working. Of course, people may not report their medical status correctly, but so long as we can verify medical disability, the disabled need not be expected to work. Similarly, the elderly are usually not expected to work.

Together, families with disabled or elderly adults account for roughly 25 percent of the poor.

For the 30-40 percent of families with a fully employed worker or the equivalent, and for the 25 percent with a disabled one, there seems little basis for any claim that the poor are not taking sufficient responsibility for themselves. Most of the remaining two-parent families fall into a more ambiguous class: those who report they did not work more because they could not find work. The difficult question is whether they could have worked if they were highly motivated to do so.

There are many indications that the bulk of the problem is true unemployment. We have already noted that poverty among stable two-parent families without disabled adults tends to be short-lived. Families do eventually find work. Moreover, even in years when the families are poor, the husband worked at least part of the year in 80 percent of the homes. Finally, we have already seen that the number of unemployed poor persons is highly sensitive to economic conditions. Poverty rates are drastically lower in prosperous times and in prosperous states.

It seems ludicrous in the face of this evidence to say that anything but a tiny minority of two-parent families could possibly have distorted values or that they are no longer part of the American mainstream. A large fraction have one adult who is already working fully or who is disabled. Most of the remainder had someone who worked at least part of the year. And most stable two-parent families who experience poverty are poor for a relatively short period of time.

Should the Government Do Something Different?

The current system of income security is a patchwork of programs typically geared to help people who have a verifiable reason for being out of work, such as disability or job loss. Social Security is available to the disabled and the elderly with work experience. Supplemental Security is available on an income-tested basis to the disabled and elderly who do not have much work experience. Worker's compensation provides some security for workers injured on the job. Unemployment insurance protects the experienced unemployed, though the duration of benefits is usually limited to six months or less. In many states a very low-income family with an unemployed primary worker can qualify for welfare. And any low-income family can get food stamps.

There is logic in this system. The disabled cannot work and ought to be taken care of. If unemployment is the result of layoffs, short-term "insurance" seems appropriate. Food stamps provides a floor for all families regardless of the cause of their troubles.

But major flaws remain. At times it seems that our social welfare system is upside down. The people who get the most money and who are most likely to be lifted out of poverty by government benefits are the disabled—the group that does not work at all. The unemployed and partially working poor are helped somewhat. Most importantly, the fully working poor are helped hardly at all.

If society expects work, then it ought to insure that work
pays off. The notion that a person would do better if he were
disabled than if he or she worked all the time challenges our
basic values of work and autonomy. If we want to minimize
the incentives for family dissolution and to encourage the con-
tinuation of two-parent working families, then we ought to
insure the security of such families. If we are going to emphasize responsibility in our rhetoric, then those people who
clearly are behaving responsibly ought to be able to achieve
a minimal standard of living without relying on stigmatizing
or degrading supports. Those who are clearly part of the working mainstream ought to be part of the economic mainstream.
    There are several things to do that can help a great deal.

Medical Protection for All Poor Persons

Large portions of the two-parent poor are left entirely without
medical protection. Contrary to popular belief, Medicaid does
not cover all of the poor. Working poor families almost never
qualify, and families with an unemployed parent are often excluded. Low-wage jobs often offer no insurance. When they
lose their jobs, the unemployed often lose any benefits they
formerly had. Among the fully working poor and unemployed
in 1984, roughly 40 percent reported no coverage. If persons
in these families become sick, they must go heavily into debt,
seek help at county hospitals, rely on charity, or get help from
friends or relief organizations.
    Medical benefits are unlikely to interfere with any incen-
tive to work—you cannot eat them or trade them for other
items. Such protection tends to integrate rather than to isolate
the poor. Medical insurance protects families from the financial burden of largely unavoidable but potentially devastating
medical conditions. I see no interpretation of our society's
values that justifies such stinginess. At a recent Ford Foundation conference, authors from major "think tanks" rang-
ing from the far right to the far left were asked to design a
social welfare system from scratch. It was striking to me that
one of the few things nearly everyone could agree upon was
that medical protection ought to be provided for all the poor.

There are many different ways in which this might be done, including requiring all employers to offer protection, setting up statewide insurance pools for the poor, and expanding Medicaid. Each has its advantages and disadvantages. Any plan will cost more money, though many of these costs are borne by the public indirectly when hospitals provide free or uncompensated care. But in a time when competition is forcing doctors and hospitals to be more cost conscious, the very people who are behaving most responsibly for the least reward—the fully working poor—are likely to be squeezed out.

Non-Welfare Help for the Working Poor

The fully working poor need to be put in a position in which they can support their families at or near the poverty line. Yet the last thing one would want to do is to put such families on welfare. The negative income tax experiments showed that such families did reduce their work efforts somewhat when they were placed in a welfare-like system. Moreover, the low reported use of food stamps suggests that the poor themselves are not interested in a stigmatizing and invasive welfare-like support.

Fortunately, there are non-welfare alternatives that are likely to have far smaller adverse effects. Families with fully working adults are poor because their wages are too low. The federal minimum wage has not changed from $3.35 since 1981, even though inflation has pushed prices (and the poverty level) up by 30 percent over this period. The arguments for or against a minimum wage are so well developed and positions are so entrenched that further discussion here will add little. Many observers are concerned that increases may reduce employment, and most analyses do show that some reductions do occur. Moreover, the vast majority of people earning the minimum wage are not poor, and, for good or ill, their status would be changed along with that of the poor. I would favor a modest increase to $4 per hour. Each $.50 per hour increase in wages raises the annual earnings of a full-time, full-year worker by $1,000.

An alternative that is more appealing to economists is to offer a carefully targeted wage subsidy of the sort advocated most recently by Robert Lerman at Brandeis University. A household could designate a principal earner (or the wage rate of two workers might be averaged). That person's wages would be subsidized if they were below some level. This plan would increase the reward for work. The more a subsidized worker worked, the more he would be paid. Since benefits would be paid only for traditional work, the subsidy would discourage participation in the underground economy. It could be administered by the employer and could even be included in the paycheck. Experimental results suggest that such a plan might well encourage work, while simultaneously increasing the incomes of the working poor.

A variation on this theme, as proposed by Robert Reischauer, would be to expand the earned income tax credit and allow it to vary by family size. The tax credit acts as a subsidy for the earnings of people at low incomes. Those with no earnings get nothing. Those with modest earnings get more. A general expansion of the credit and the addition of an adjustment for family size would help protect larger families while encouraging low-income workers with families to return to work. One appealing feature of this plan is that it requires no new agency or bureaucracy for its administration. Poor families submit tax forms like everyone else. With an earned income tax credit, many would get more back from the government than they paid to it.

The effects are not identical to a wage subsidy. The tax credit system would also help poor families in which someone worked at a reasonably well-paying job for part of the year. Their annual earnings would be low, so they would be eligible for an earned income tax credit, even though their average wage for the period when they were working was high. For these families the overall effects on work would be somewhat more ambiguous.

Another way in which the tax system could help would be to convert the current deduction for children into a refundable tax credit. Thus, for example, every parent might receive a

$500-750 tax credit for each child. Such a credit surely would not be enough to encourage families to have more children, and it would be a minor disincentive to work, but it would help families, particularly large families, to meet their needs.

The exact specifics can be the subject of political give and take, guided in part by more detailed experimentation and analysis. The essential point is that there are clear and appealing ways to help the fully working poor. If society is going to worry about responsibility among the poor, it ought to insure that the working poor, those for whom there is no question of irresponsibility, are part of the economic mainstream.

Transitional Support for the Unemployed

If we provided medical care for all of the poor and provided more non-welfare supports to the fully working poor, we would make major progress in our attempts to reduce poverty and insecurity while encouraging work and responsibility.

But there would still be unemployed workers who could not qualify for unemployment insurance or who had exhausted their benefits. For these persons, the problem is somewhat more difficult. Whether their plight merits protection by a significant expansion of the welfare system is controversial, particularly since poverty in stable two-parent homes tends to be relatively temporary. The fear is that families would become dependent or that working families would do no better than those on such an expanded welfare system.

Still, it seems questionable to decry government policies as promoting single-parent families if we are unwilling to provide some protection to two-parent families who are out of work. One possibility is to provide government jobs. Government jobs would lessen concerns about dependency on a welfare type of system, but a jobs-based strategy would be both expensive and controversial. Many worry that a jobs program would depress wages, create an administrative nightmare, and do little to enhance the long-term prospects of people who are out of work.

A more plausible strategy would be to offer a short-term

transitional assistance program for those who have been missed by the safety net of disability and unemployment insurance. The program could offer training and education, paying a stipend as long as the family participated in the training or could demonstrate participation in other activities to help its situation, but in no case would the benefits extend beyond a specified period such as 18 to 24 months. This system could also be extended to people with short-term illnesses or disabilities who do not qualify for disability insurance, but who nonetheless are limited in their ability to work.

Such a strategy is in keeping with the findings reported earlier that show that most stable two-parent families that experience poverty are poor for a relatively short period of time. By linking training and retraining to benefits, the program could tie into existing manpower programs and offer a more comprehensive system of support and investment in human resources.

There is now strong sentiment in favor of extending eligibility for the Aid to Families with Dependent Children (AFDC) welfare program to all two-parent families in which the principal earner is unemployed. States are now required to offer such support only to single parents and to those with a disabled primary earner. The states have the option of extending AFDC to the unemployed but not all states have elected to do so. The AFDC-UP (Unemployed Parent) program, as it is called, could be required in all states.

Although such a move is clearly a step in the right direction, I believe it would be far preferable to move toward a program that is more generous but limited in duration. AFDC benefit levels are frightfully low and they will remain so as long as people perceive welfare as allowing recipients to become dependent. I doubt that unemployment insurance would be very popular if it lasted forever. Moreover, any program designed both to provide for long-term income maintenance and to help clients move into independence must wrestle with the competing goals of insuring economic security and encouraging independence.

A program that is limited in duration simply does not allow for dependence, and its goals are quite clear. The perception of the program by both the poor and the non-poor is likely to be far more favorable if it is viewed as temporary insurance and a stepping stone to work, rather than an alternative to employment. Moreover, a program with an eventual end puts pressure on both clients and administrators to use it as a bridge, as a transition into self-support and independence.

Jobs for the Long-Term Unemployed

If the proposals suggested so far were adopted, the results presented in this paper suggest that there would be relatively few two-parent families left in severe poverty. There would no doubt be situations, though, in which people still will not have been able to find work. For this relatively small group of people, it would make sense to create a government jobs program that paid the minimum wage.

If one is going to insist that families with healthy adults support themselves through work, and if cash assistance is limited in duration, then society needs to offer a way for people who have not been able to find work to support themselves. Jobs are the obvious solution. If the jobs are limited to those who have been through the transitional program and wages are kept low, there seems little danger that many private jobs will be displaced or that the cost will be great. A jobs program also puts families in a position in which they can support themselves— however meagerly—using the route society deems most desirable: work.

There may be a few people who cannot work at even the most modest jobs without far more training and education. The whole point of the transitional assistance program would be to get these people the training they need. If after that period, work is still unlikely, one could imagine other systems of more intensive training/treatment that can be offered in place of the jobs program. But the evidence suggests that such people would be few. It is inappropriate and illogical to design the whole support/security system around a small group that does not quite fit. They ought to be treated individually.

These suggestions are based on the finding that there are many people who are unequivocally behaving responsibly and on the philosophical premise that such people deserve to be able to support themselves and to be assured of medical protection without having to rely on invasive or degrading government assistance. For the disabled, disability protection works rather well; for the working poor, wage or earned income supports look desirable. There is a smaller group of people who appear to be unemployed in the true sense of the term, and they deserve short-term assistance in the form of transitional services. But for the poor and non-poor alike, it does not seem desirable for such assistance to be unlimited. For the small number of families with employable adults who need longer-term sources of income support, jobs seem to be the appropriate tool. And for everyone medical protection ought to be assured in some way.

Families Headed
by Women

Unfortunately, the poverty of female-headed families defies the "easy" descriptions and prescriptions that are possible for the two-parent poor. Before asking why single-parent families are poor so often, we ought first to consider why the number of children in female-headed families has grown so much. There is a widespread perception that the main reason that female-headed families have grown so much is that welfare benefits have encouraged family dissolution and out-of-wedlock births.

It is a shock to many people, therefore, to discover that in the period since the early 1970s, during which there has been dramatic growth in the number of children in female-headed families, the number of children on AFDC, the primary welfare program for single parents, has actually fallen rather considerably! One finds this pattern for both black and white children. If people were splitting up or having babies more and more often in order to get welfare benefits or even if welfare was just a contributing means of support, the number of children on AFDC should have grown, not fallen.

The reason that the number on AFDC fell was that after dramatic increases in the benefits and liberalization in the eligibility rules in the mid- to late 1960s, benefits for AFDC have steadily *fallen* and eligibility rules tightened. After adjustment for inflation, the combined value of AFDC and food stamps has fallen at least 25 percent since the early 1970s.

And even though there is enormous variation in welfare benefits among various states, there is little or no correlation between benefit levels and the number of children in female-headed families.

There is no consensus on what is causing the changes in family structure in our society. It seems likely that the increased independence of both women and men has played a role. Many argue that opportunities for women have risen faster than those for men. Changing norms and expectations surely have played a role. In the black community, most of the changes can be traced to declines in marriage. For some reason, marriage has declined sharply among young blacks. William Julius Wilson has offered the most convincing explanation for this phenomenon. Employment among young black men has also declined sharply. Marriage looks less attractive to both parties. And in the ghettos of America the answer is no doubt even more complicated. Women with little hope of achieving middle-class status, with little control and limited affection in their lives, with few marriageable men around, may see motherhood as one of the few ways to gain some measure of identity and self-worth.

Yet, it is important to emphasize that no one really understands what has caused the changes in American society. This is the frustrating state of the current research. In such a situation it is tempting to look for single easy answers, like welfare. Yet there are no widely cited or highly respected studies that have found that welfare has had much of an effect. One must always be cautious, and new evidence may eventually overturn current results. What is clear, and even Murray agrees with this proposition, is that modest changes in the welfare system are unlikely to have any effect on the number of children in single-parent homes.

One is also left with a question of what we should do even if we did believe that welfare influenced the formation of families. Murray argues for the complete elimination of all social welfare supports. We have already seen just how poor such families are. Should we sacrifice this generation of children hoping that the next generation will not be born?

Such an approach seems extraordinarily harsh. And no one has provided the slightest evidence that the genie can be put back into the bottle. Nevertheless, one surely must pay attention to the incentives the system is creating. Even though there is little evidence about family formation incentives, they deserve explicit consideration in any income-support arrangement.

Why Are Single Mothers Poor?

The poverty of two-parent families could easily be traced to economic conditions. The poverty of female heads of family is more complicated. Table 4 shows that low wages and unemployment clearly play important roles in the poverty of female family heads. Some 6.4 percent are already working full time all year; for them the problem is clearly low wages.

Table 4

Main Reason Why Poor* Female Heads of Households with Children Did Not Work More During 1984

Already Working Full Year	
Full Time	7.9%
Part Time	5.4%
Worked Part of the Year,	
But Couldn't Find Work	
During the Remainder	10.6%
Unable to Find Work At All	7.7%
Ill or Disabled	10.8%
Taking Care of House/Children	47.4%
Retired	2.0%
In School	3.9%
Other	4.2%
TOTAL	100.0%

* Family income not counting government transfers is below the poverty line.
Source: Special Tabulations of the Current Population Survey, 1984.

Another 22 percent report wanting to work more but are unable to find work. And 5 percent work full year, part time and thus were not asked about why they did not work more. In all, perhaps one-third of all female heads of family report low wages or a lack of jobs as the primary reason for their low earnings (as opposed to 72 percent of male heads). Another 12.8 percent point to illness, disability, or retirement as limiting their capacity for work.

But by far the biggest reason for not working more is the "taking care of house/children." We are inevitably confronted with the question of how such reports are to be interpreted. We turn to that discussion below. No doubt, a portion of the group that reports family responsibilities might work if better opportunities were available. Generally, we would not expect them to be as readily influenced by economic conditions alone as two-parent families for whom wages and unemployment were the most important reported reasons for poverty.

Since limited economic opportunity and wages remain an important direct cause of poverty for families headed by women, one would expect that variations in the poverty rate of female family heads would be largely the result of economic variables. Indeed, one finds that the earnings of full-year, full-time female workers, and the unemployment rate, do predict year-to-year variations in poverty rates reasonably well. (Figure 2.) But even in the best of times, poverty rates remain very high. And in spite of major variations in economic conditions during the 1970s and 1980s, the poverty level was relatively flat. It seems quite obvious that in the short run economic growth and reductions in unemployment will reduce only a modest portion of the poverty of female-headed families. The problem of poverty for single parents runs deeper than the current level of wages and unemployment.

Massachusetts once again offers a helpful example. Whereas the pre-transfer poverty rate for two-parent families in the state was half of the national average, the rate for single-parent families is 46.2 percent, close to the national average of 51.9 percent. Even in good economic times the bulk of the problem remains.

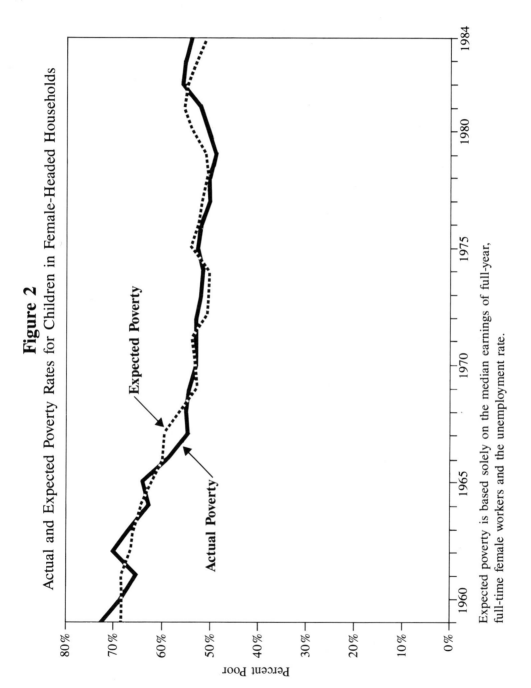

Figure 2

Actual and Expected Poverty Rates for Children in Female-Headed Households

Expected poverty is based solely on the median earnings of full-year, full-time female workers and the unemployment rate.

"Trickle down" will not work nearly as well for single-parent families as it does for two-parent homes. The clear implication is that if strong economic growth were to persist for a decade, pushing wages up and unemployment down, the poverty of two-parent families would be almost eliminated, but the poverty of single-parent families would remain high. Thus in the future it seems likely that an increasing proportion of poor children will be living in single-parent families, even if the number of children in single-parent families remains the same.[9] A greater fraction of poor two-parent families are helped by economic growth. Single parents will be left behind.

Should Single Mothers Do More for Themselves?

Single mothers are under attack now as failing to meet their responsibilities to society and to their children. In a simpler time, mothers were expected to be mainly the nurturer and homemaker for the family. Economic support came from a husband. When our current program of aid to single parents was devised, it seemed unreasonable to expect women to provide both the economic and the social support of the family. AFDC was a program for widows, women with disabled husbands, and a small number of families abandoned by the father.

Two trends have overtaken the system: the dramatic increase in the number of women who are female heads of households for more "voluntary" reasons, such as divorce, separation, and childbirth, and the equally dramatic increase in the work of married mothers. As a result, it no longer seems as appropriate for single mothers "only" to raise their children.

But what are reasonable expectations for single mothers? In two-parent families, husbands usually work full year, full time. Wives occasionally work full year and full time, more often work part time, and frequently do not work at all. In essence, then, the question boils down to this: Do we expect female family heads to work like husbands or like wives?

If single mothers are to be self-supporting, they will have to work as much as husbands, and even then many would be poor. We have already seen that many husbands cannot insure that family income will exceed the poverty line by working fully. For women, wages are still lower. Yet some 90 percent of single mothers who do work full time escape poverty, though one would expect those with the greatest earning potential to be the most likely to work. Others are not likely to be so fortunate.

On the other hand, wives, like single mothers, are increasingly called upon to fill both provider and child-rearing roles. But given the limited opportunities, the cost of day care, the need to maintain the household, and the felt need to stay home with the children, only 27 percent of married mothers work full year, full time. Almost 40 percent work part time. The remaining third do not work at all.

There are strong arguments to be made for expecting some work and support from single mothers. Both feminists and psychologists argue that some work can be a very valuable thing for both women and child. Work can offer a woman a measure of independence and control, and it can serve as a stepping stone to a more secure future. Some authors also express concern about children raised for long periods of time in a home where no one does any labor-market work. The current welfare system actually expects little work from welfare mothers (though it offers very low welfare benefits in exchange). A few children literally spend their entire lives on welfare and in homes where mothers hardly ever work for pay. I found in previous work that while welfare serves as a temporary bridge for a great many women, for an important minority (perhaps 25 percent of those who ever use it) welfare support goes on for ten years or more. Such dependence seems troubling for all involved.

At the same time it seems both impractical and unfair to expect all single mothers to work all the time. It is easy to argue that the burdens of work are greater for a single mother than for a married mother. And the question of what is best for the children remains. Society may be willing to expect all single mothers to work some, except perhaps those with very young children. But to insist that all single mothers ought to work all the time just to maintain their families at the poverty line seems absurd and extraordinarily harsh, particularly when one remembers that at least half of all our children (and thus roughly half of all married mothers) will spend some period in single-parent homes. The only fair and practical minimum expectation would seem to be part-time work. Those who are willing and able to work more ought to be encouraged to do so. For a minimal income, though, working half or two-thirds of the time would seem to be enough.

Yet our current economic/welfare system offers women just two choices: they can work all the time or they can be on welfare. Part-time work alone does not provide enough money to support a family. And under the present system, it does not pay financially to work part time. After four months, the welfare check is reduced by as much as the new income. Given these choices, single mothers do tend either to work fully or not at all. Whereas part-time work is the most common choice for wives, it is the least common for female family heads. Somehow it seems that we need to offer a third choice, a way for a woman to work part time yet avoid becoming embroiled in the welfare system with its unpleasant treatment, connotations of failure, and endless rules and regulations. We shall consider the alternatives shortly.

There is a second group whose responsibility might be questioned: absent parents—usually absent fathers. Half of the single mothers do not even receive a court-ordered payment of child support. Only 40 percent of separated women have them, and among never-married mothers, only 17 percent receive payments. Moreover, of those with awards, only half received the full amount of payments while one-quarter received nothing. There is not time in this paper to discuss the multitude of issues surrounding child support. The bottom line is quite simple: only one-third of all female family heads with children report receiving any child-support payments at all. Among poor female family heads, the figure is just 20 percent.

The reasons for these failures will be discussed in the next section. Whatever the reasons, however, the message being sent out is quite clear: absent parents are not responsible for supporting their children. And the fathers of children born out of wedlock certainly seem to bear almost no legally enforced responsibilities—91 percent paid nothing in child support. I suspect that most Americans would find this state of affairs highly offensive. The issue here is not economics, it is responsibility. It is a matter of right and wrong.

We are increasingly asking single mothers to provide both financial and social support for their children. Society ought to enforce the same obligation on absent fathers (and absent mothers for that matter). All current and prospective parents ought to know that except in the most extreme circumstances, they have an obligation to share a portion of whatever income they have with all of their children, whether they are absent from home or not.

Should Government Do Something Different?
Single parents can now get unemployment insurance or disability protection if they qualify. But relatively few report receiving it. The main source of support is AFDC. AFDC is also the program that virtually everyone hates. AFDC seems to be the worst of all worlds. For economic subsistence, many single mothers are forced into a system that offers relatively modest support (well below the poverty line in most areas) and benefits have fallen sharply over the past decade. The system itself is often a nightmare of rules and regulations for clients and administrators alike. Welfare is often described by recipients as humiliating and destructive. It isolates single mothers and labels them as failures who are wards of the state.

Yet in spite of the unpleasantness of the experience and often ridiculously low benefits, there clearly are people who stay on welfare for years. Both conservatives and liberals sometimes argue that the whole system robs the poor of their confidence, initiative, and self-esteem, though the reasons offered are usually quite different. AFDC seems an awkward compromise that simply does not work. It takes some of our most precious values—people ought to be self-supporting; people ought to be treated with dignity and respect; families (preferably two-parent families) ought to provide for and raise the children; people ought to be held responsible for their actions; people ought to be integrated into the society, not isolated from it — and puts them into terrible conflict.

Social Security causes no such value conflicts. It provides benefits to virtually all old persons, and the benefits are tied to past work. There is no question of responsibility, self-support, family, isolation, or stigma. Benefits were earned through hard work and granted for old age. No wonder AFDC is tossed about on the current political winds, while Social Security is protected even in the most stringent times. One would hope that something much more compatible with our values and aspirations might replace AFDC.

Of course, one solution would be to avoid the problem entirely by reducing the number of single-parent families. There are a number of ways in which government might try to do that. It could make things even more unpleasant for single-parent families by cutting meager welfare benefits still further. We have already seen that a child raised entirely in a single-parent home is likely to be poor and dependent throughout childhood. Our society is reluctant to visit the "sins" of the mother on the child. And the majority of people who ever get welfare use it for only a short period of time. They do not deserve this penalty. In any case, we have already tried cutting welfare benefits dramatically in the past decade, and there was no perceptible effect on single-parent families.

We could try to improve the situation for two-parent families (or childless persons) and thereby make marriage more attractive and divorce/separation relatively less so. I have already discussed some methods for doing that. Similarly, we could improve the employment situation for young people so that marriage, particularly in the black community, would be more attractive and practical.

We can work desperately hard to educate young people about the impact of childbearing. We could increase knowledge about and the availability of contraception. We could promote the use of clinics in schools, and improve the availability of birth control and abortion. Such measures are controversial. They often raise other difficult value questions. And many have not been carefully validated as effective. But they remain a logical, straightforward, and relatively inexpensive approach to the problem of single parenthood.

Finally we could make things worse for absent fathers by imposing additional obligations on them, which might cause them to think twice before fathering a child (or before they divorce or separate). Imposing additional obligations on a group that is not now doing its fair share would seem the least controversial of the measures. And it may come closest to influencing the decisions of those whose behavior must be changed.

Frankly, I am skeptical that any of these will make a large difference in the number of children being raised in single-parent homes. It must be remembered that half of all the children born today will spend some time in a single-parent home. Such a trend is not likely to be snuffed out by tampering with welfare or child support. Still, it should be clear that if one is seeking to reduce the frequency with which children are raised in single-parent homes, there are alternatives to making life worse for single mothers.

Ultimately, we must confront the economic situation of single mothers. With so many children likely to spend some time in a single-parent home, the economic situation of such homes is fundamental to the economic condition of our children. Ideally, we would like to do something to improve their economic condition, to encourage more work and more personal control, to reduce dependency—but we would like to do so in a way that does not encourage the formation of more such households.

Current proposals for change will help, but they do not really solve the problem. "Workfare" increases the obligations of single mothers but such a program still leaves single mothers with two choices: work all the time or be on welfare/workfare. It also ignores the fact that many women come onto AFDC for a relatively short time. It seems unnecessary and even undesirable to insist on work from all single mothers as soon as they enter the program. And workfare does not improve a woman's options so much as it increases her obligations. It leaves workfare mothers almost as isolated from the mainstream as welfare does. All the programs that have been carefully evaluated to date have shown only very modest success in moving welfare mothers into work more quickly than they would have moved on their own. More child care and more training can help, but these also do not change the basic choices.

I believe there is a better alternative. It is derived in large part from the work of Irwin Garfinkel and from the experiments being tried by the state of Wisconsin. It starts with a serious reform of our current child-support system.

Child-Support Assurance

At present, child-support awards, when they are made at all, are usually made in fixed dollar terms and they largely reflect current circumstances. In inflationary times, the real value of these payments can fall quite dramatically. Judges have enormous discretion, so even when awards are made they vary widely. And since payments reflect present conditions of the parties at the time of the award, it often makes little sense to bring a young absent father to court since he often has very little money initially. Yet few men remain penniless their entire lives. Not finding the men immediately makes identification much more difficult, and the likelihood of imposing child-support obligations later becomes remote.

At present it is the woman's responsibility to press for court proceedings (except in the case in which the state pursues the fathers of children on welfare), and to initiate new ones if the father fails to pay or if the mother believes higher payments are warranted. The expense, the unpleasantness, the uncertainty, and frequently the desire to maintain contact with the father all mitigate against child-support awards and enforcement.

And so the present system ends up sending the clear signal that fathers will not necessarily be held accountable for some support of their children. It leaves many children completely reliant on one parent for financial support. Even those mothers with awards cannot count on the money.

The child-support assurance plan such as that being experimented with in Wisconsin and elsewhere would solve virtually all of these problems by creating a more comprehensive and uniform system. And it would displace a large part of the current welfare system. It would consist of a four-part reform:

• Society would commit itself to identifying every father and mother. For the future, the Social Security numbers of both parents ought to appear on a child's birth certificate. Most experts claim that getting the father's name is not difficult and proving paternity is quite feasible as well. What can be more difficult is finding the father years later if one does not have a Social Security number. Mothers who did not cooperate would lose eligibility for child-support assurance payments, though they could be excused through court order.

• Each absent parent would be expected to contribute a portion of his or her income (earnings), which would vary with the number of children. There would be a roughly uniform formula for child support. Wisconsin uses a plan calling for 17 percent of income for one child, 25 percent for two, up to 34 percent for five or more children. Courts could deviate from this if they were justified by circumstance. Such a formula would not fully take into account current circumstances, but then our tax system is based on an identical system. Imagine what would happen if we tried to base taxes on all individual conditions.

• All payments would be collected by employers just as Social Security taxes are collected. Indeed, it could be part of the Social Security system. The government would then send this money to the custodial parent. All absent parents would be included in the system, not just those who had been delinquent.

• In cases in which the earnings of the absent parent were insufficient to provide some minimum level of child support, say $1500 per child, the government would provide that minimum. In effect, when the father failed in his obligation to provide sufficient income for child support, the government would insure that his children get at least some minimum amount.

There is not space available to discuss many of the pros and cons of uniform guaranteed child support here. But it has many very appealing features. It would reform the most serious abuses of the present system. It would hold fathers accountable and it would take the mothers out of the business of enforcing child support. Particularly if combined with an expanded earned income tax credit and a refundable tax credit for children, it can put women in a position in which child support (which is seen as the *father's* obligation) plus a part-time job could allow a family to support itself above the poverty line.

Single parents and their children would be part of a social insurance type of child-support system that covered all separated parents, not just the poor. It would be a system that protected all children. This would be a logical way to cope with the emerging majority of children who spend time in single-parent homes.

With at least a minimum level of child support guaranteed, a mother need never see a welfare office if she can find part-time work. Child support becomes an income supplement. She can support her family and raise them, and when the government must supplement the father's contribution to insure a minimum level of child support, it is to cover the failure of the father to do his share, not because the mother has failed.

To some this system may seem a disguised AFDC program. The money that used to come in the form of a welfare check now comes as a minimum child-support payment. The resemblance is merely superficial. In the welfare system, when a woman starts earning money, her welfare check is reduced, often dollar for dollar with her earnings. In extreme contrast, the support payments would reflect the absent parent's obligation and contribution (guaranteed by the government). The check would not be affected by the mother's work. She would keep every dollar of her earnings. Nor would a woman have to visit a welfare office, report all her earnings, be investigated by caseworkers, or be treated as a failure in order to get her child support.

Most importantly, this would be a system for all separated families and parents. Children at all ends of the income spectrum would have much better protection in the event that families split up. The system would tend to integrate poor single mothers rather than isolate them. Poor single mothers would get a child-support check reflecting government collections (and any subsidy) just as middle- and upper-income women would. The system could emerge as more like the Social Security system than like welfare. Social Security also provides minimum benefits and has little income testing. It is popular in part because it covers the whole population.

Most amazing of all, according to its architects, this system would improve the well-being of single mothers without increasing the cost of assistance at all. Increased costs for the minimum child-support protection would be offset by savings in AFDC and increased collections from fathers.

There are some disadvantages. Any system that treats people in a relatively uniform manner will not take full account of individual circumstances. Some absent parents will argue that their position is in fact worse than that of the custodial parent. Going after every absent parent may be costly. But the present system is absurd. It leaves an enormous number of children completely unsupported. And it sends a clear message about parental responsibility, particularly to those who father children out of wedlock.

The appeal of the child-support assurance system is that it puts single mothers in a vastly more realistic position to become self-supporting, integrates them into the mainstream insurance/protection system, and simultaneously reinforces the responsibility of absent fathers for the support of their children. The increased responsibility may even serve as a deterrent to the fathering of children outside of marriage. It comes close to offering something for nothing. More responsibility, more options, more independence, with no more money.

Short-Term Transitional Support, Jobs for Long-Term Support

Not all women will find part-time work immediately. And some mothers will still prefer to stay at home with their children. We will continue to need some sort of welfare/income support for single mothers. With the child-support assurance in place though, one could provide assistance using something similar to or identical to the transitional short-term and employment-based, long-term support system described for two-parent families.

Currently welfare serves two roles: it is a temporary bridge for many, and it is a source of long-term income support for others. The majority of users do not stay on welfare for more than a few years, but a smaller number use it for a very long period of time. The mixed goals imply mixed messages to recipients, administrators, and the public. The goals can conflict sharply. The more generous the long-term support the less incentive there is to become self-supporting. Public support is diminished by the perception that the system is encouraging dependence and legitimizing an underclass.

The simplest and most logical solution is to separate the two functions cleanly. Single mothers would first enter a transitional support plan similar (identical?) to the one offered to two-parent families. The program might last 18-36 months (depending on the age of the children). During that period women could elect to participate in a variety of training and education programs. Day care would be provided along with other services. And reasonably generous income support would be offered that would supplement the child-support payments. The program would seek to offer dignity, personal investments, and choice. However, the support would not last indefinitely. After the benefit period was used up, the only available source of support would be a jobs program, again similar to that for two-parent families. Long-term income maintenance would be in the form of work, not welfare. With the child-support assurance plan in place, such women would only need to work part time to support their family. Just as in the case of two-parent families, there will be people who need special, intensive services, who somehow do not qualify for the disability programs but who cannot make it on their own. They need to be treated on a special case-by-case basis. They should not be allowed to drive the shape of the whole social welfare system.

In some respects this transitional support plan followed by a jobs package is similar to current welfare reform proposals and to some state programs, such as California's GAIN program, which require some job search or training followed by workfare for welfare recipients. These proposals may offer a workable alternative. They move in the right direction. Yet I believe that it is essential to make clear to all those concerned, both recipients and the public, that the core support program is a transitional one. The program is generous but limited in time. Eventually the person will have to go to work. Cash assistance would go to those in transition. Work would go to those needing long-term support. Both the transitional support and the jobs program seem likely to be more demanding and effective and more likely to have a better image among poor and non-poor alike, if the missions and expectations are divided and clear.

It should be noted that the child-support assurance system is critical to the success of any plan of this sort. Unless single mothers are put in a position whereby they can realistically be self-supporting while working half or two-thirds time, society cannot resolve the dilemma of whether single mothers ought to work all the time. If single mothers are going to fulfill both nurturing and economic support roles, if society is going to expect them to take more responsibility for their families, then they must be given more realistic alternatives, options, and opportunities.

A Brief Note about America's Ghettos

There really is a third group that merits attention: the ghetto poor. In my book, I spend considerable time discussing the special situation one finds in the poorest neighborhoods of our central cities. In this paper, I want to comment on these problems only briefly. What one sees in ghetto neighborhoods is distressing. Ghetto areas deserve special and intensive attention. But the ghetto residents Nicholas Lehman writes about and who spoke on Bill Moyer's television special must not become our new stereotypic image of the poor. Minorities living in the poorest neighborhoods (those with a poverty rate of 40 percent or more) in the top 100 central cities constitute only 6 percent of the poor. No matter what one sees in these neighborhoods, the entirety of social policy certainly should not be be based on the problems of that population.

What one sees in America's ghettos is concentration, as poor people are crowded together; isolation, as middle-class families move out; deprivation, as children grow up poor; inferior education, as central city schools decay; and limited opportunity, as low-skill jobs evaporate or move out of the city. Crime and drugs add additional elements. Children living in this environment see few role models, limited opportunity, a poor educational system, intimidating yet respected criminals, and a decaying infrastructure. At best, such children are left with despair. They see no opportunity of joining the mainstream they see in abundance on television. They have little reason to believe that something they do can change

49

their lives, since all their friends are poor. Virtually none have jobs. Frankly, if pathologies did not develop in an environment as horrendous as this, it would be a modern miracle. A group that is so isolated geographically, economically, and socially will become an underclass.

Charles Murray claims all this despair is the result of the elite liberal wisdom that brought us welfare rights and a don't-blame-the-victim mentality. Welfare probably played some role. It does help sustain the community. Yet only 40 percent of the families in these areas report receiving public assistance income. And the worst-off group is probably young black men, who receive no welfare.

In a context such as this, questions of why young girls get pregnant or why young people don't marry or why people don't work more seem almost trite. For a young girl who sees no chance of joining the mainstream, few sources of affection in her life, few ways to control her hostile environment, few opportunities to marry an employed and responsible man, bearing a child may seem very natural and desirable. Even if work were available, it would seem to offer little immediate chance for escape. Why should a youngster who sees the past as a series of happenstance events expect his or her actions to change the future?

The predominant impression one gets of ghetto life is of helplessness and defeatism. Conservatives claim that this results from a social welfare system that rewards the failures. What is needed for ghetto residents is a good swift kick. I suspect that swift kicks are about all that life has offered ghetto residents so far. Helplessness is born of a system in which the motivated do not succeed, a system that offers a boot to all who come by.

Glenn Loury has been prominent in proclaiming that the black community should do more to condemn illegitimacy, to demand responsibility, to instill middle-class values. And so it should. But it is hard to see how condemnation and pronouncements will really change people in such an environment. Surely the poor could do more for themselves and surely the call to self-control would have more power if people saw a real chance to escape the despair.

It seems easy to dismiss this group as irresponsible or unreachable. But the fundamental premises of our values call for people to have the opportunity to make it into the mainstream. If my children grew up in this sort of world, I cannot imagine that they would have that chance. Somehow, one must make it possible and then make it plain that the motivated do succeed and that their lives are better than the underground alternative lives that are offered in the ghetto. Probably the most important thing society needs to do is to offer hope. Eugene Lang offered such hope to a group of sixth-grade youngsters in Harlem by offering them a free college education if they made good progress in school. As seniors, virtually everyone is still in school and headed for college—in sharp contrast to all the others before them. It appears that when very young people believe they are special and when they think that they have a chance to "make it," they can and do respond. But in an environment in which there is a great deal of failure and little success, there is no reason to be hopeful.

What is not needed is many more welfare dollars delivered in the same system that now exists. These will do little to help people escape. But welfare cuts seem likely only to add to the despair. I believe that the policies I have suggested will help. They can improve opportunity, while emphasizing personal control and responsibility. They would guarantee that people could support themselves at the poverty level through work. But these policies will not solve all of the problems one finds in the ghettos.

The sad truth is that we have only glimpses of where to look for deeper and more effective answers to the problems of the ghetto poor. There will be no quick fixes, no magic silver bullets. Preschool education really does seem to make a difference. More and better opportunities can help. What we need is intensive, long-term experimentation and commitment to education, opportunity, and empowerment. If we cannot offer a real vision, a real hope to those in our most hostile neighborhoods, America may lose an important segment of its society.

Regardless of what is done for the ghettos, policy makers and the public must not get trapped into the easy image of the ghetto resident as the stereotypical poor person. There is much that can be done to improve and rationalize the way in which we help all the poor in America. The despair of the ghetto, which constitutes less than a tenth of the poor population, cannot be allowed to dominate our images.

Conclusion

"**W**ork" and "responsibility" seem to be the words with the greatest currency in this most recent push for welfare reform. It does appear that our current social welfare system has lost sight of these concepts at times. But if the society is to urge work and responsibility on its poorest citizens, then it must take responsibility for insuring that those people who are working and who are behaving responsibly can at least achieve our minimal standard of living. It must also insure that people who are willing and able to work can find a way to support themselves. Responsible security involves mutual responsibilities. Our current social welfare system treats the disabled and the elderly relatively well. It offers somewhat haphazard and often meager protection for the unemployed. It offers almost nothing for the full-time, working-poor family. It seems somewhat perverse that the poor who are working most get the least medical protection and the least income support.

People who are working "enough" and still not making it need some sort of supplements. They must have some form of guaranteed medical protections. And we need to supplement their income, not with welfare, but with non-invasive, non-degrading supports that reinforce work and personal responsibility where possible. For two-parent families, those supports could include wage subsidies, further expansion of the earned income tax credit, and changing of the current

53

tax exemption for children into a refundable tax credit. All of these avoid degrading the working poor or imposing special requirements on them. They help without welfare.

Single parents need extra support. They typically have just one person to fill the role of both breadwinner and nurturer. An obvious source of support is the absent parent. With less than one-third of absent parents contributing to their children today, it is little wonder that so many single women cannot escape poverty. A universal child-support system with money withheld by the employer from the wages of absent parents, coupled with a minimum support level insured by the government, along with wage subsidies or a refundable tax credit, can put women in a position in which those who work half time or two-thirds time really can support their families without any need for traditional welfare. Moreover, such a policy sends a clear message: both parents are responsible; both parents have an obligation to share their incomes with a child.

Most people who are not working as much as might be hoped are in the midst of a temporary crisis—either physical (temporary disability), economic (loss of a job), or personal (divorce or separation). For them the logical form of support is transitional support. Most Americans are willing to be generous, I suspect, if they do not feel their contributions are being abused. A system that is transitional and temporary sends the clear message to recipient and non-recipient alike that the aid is designed to move people into self-sufficiency, not to substitute for it.

Finally, there will be a few healthy people who will not be self-supporting even with the earned income and child-support supplements, and after they have received transitional aid. Jobs seem the appropriate form of long-term income maintenance for these people. Some may need special aid or intensive support. Those cases can be handled separately.

Responsibility and security can be combined. If we are to truly help the poor and if we are to create a social welfare system that has political credibility, it must confront both the values we honor and the realities associated with the diverse causes of poverty. It is far easier to divide and conquer poverty than to try to magically transform it with some ultimate solution.

Notes

1. In preparing this paper, I have received very helpful comments from Regina Aragon, Mary Jo Bane, Gordon Berlin, Tom Kane, Richard Nathan, Robert Reischauer, and participants at a September 1986 conference.

2. The PSID is a survey that has followed 5,000 American families annually since 1967. I used the fifteen-year sample from this survey. All results are weighted.

3. The data I report are averages for children born between 1967 and 1973 who are followed for the first ten years after their birth. For simplicity of discussion, I report the data as though they represent a single year's birth cohort.

4. There really are three types of families: two-parent families, single-parent families headed by a woman, and single-parent families headed by a man. The last group is so small (2 percent of children) that they do not merit separate discussion. Their behavior looks almost like that of husbands in two-parent families throughout this paper. In language that the Census has now discarded as obsolete, the people classified here as living in two-parent homes are actually living in families with a "male head."

5. Even this figure is optimistic. Family status is actually determined just once a year at the time of the survey. Some of those listed as having always been in a two-parent home, may have been in a single-parent home for part of the year that did not happen to fall on the survey date. And some of

those who were always in a two-parent home, may not have had the same two parents throughout this period.

6. Unlike the other numbers reported in this paper, these are for the officially defined poor, the only ones available from published data. In defining official poverty, government transfers are added before comparing family income to the poverty line. In this paper such transfers are not added so as to provide a sense of what people are doing on their own.

7. The actual rule for disability is that the person be unable to work for at least the next twelve months.

8. Unlike the other numbers and tables in this paper, the poverty rates shown here and in Figure 2 are post-transfer levels (the official method for calculating poverty). For my purposes, I would prefer to have a figure showing pre-transfer poverty levels. Unfortunately, such data are not available for this entire time period. In years where data are available, the results are very similar to those found in Figure 1.

9. This is in fact what happened between 1959 and 1969. Children in female-headed homes went from being 25 percent of the poor to almost 50 percent of the poor, even though the proportion of children in female-headed homes changed little. Economic growth pushed a far greater proportion of the two-parent poor families out of poverty.

David T. Ellwood, associate professor of public policy at the John F. Kennedy School of Government, Harvard University, is a labor economist who specializes in the problems of the poor and the disadvantaged and in policies designed to help them. He is the author of studies of the causes of poverty, the effect of welfare on family structures, the causes and consequences of youth unemployment, and welfare reform. Professor Ellwood is on the Advisory Board for the Work and Welfare Demonstrations being evaluated by Manpower Demonstration Research Corporation, and is a faculty research fellow at the National Bureau of Economic Research.